Baptism: Mode and Design

by

Rev. W.B. Godbey, A.M

First Fruits Press
Wilmore,
Kentucky c2017

Baptism: mode and design. By W.B. Godbey.
First Fruits Press, © 2017

ISBN: 9781621717454 (print), 9781621717546 (digital), 9781621717553 (kindle)

Digital version at http://place.asburyseminary.edu/godbey/9/

For all other uses, contact:

First Fruits Press
B.L. Fisher Library
Asbury Theological Seminary
204 N. Lexington Ave.
Wilmore, KY 40390
http://place.asburyseminary.edu/firstfruits

Godbey, W. B. (William Baxter), 1833-1920.
  Baptism : mode and design / by W.B. Godbey. – Wilmore, KY : First Fruits Press, ©2017.
    109 pages ; cm.
    Reprint. Previously published: Louisville, Ky. : Pentecostal Publishing Co., 1883
    ISBN: 9781621717454 (pbk.)
    1. Baptism. I. Title.
        BV811.5.G633 2017   265.1

Cover design by Jon Ramsey

asburyseminary.edu
800.2ASBURY
204 North Lexington Avenue
Wilmore, Kentucky 40390

First Fruits
THE ACADEMIC OPEN PRESS OF ASBURY SEMINARY

First Fruits Press
The Academic Open Press of Asbury Theological Seminary
204 N. Lexington Ave., Wilmore, KY 40390
859-858-2236
first.fruits@asburyseminary.edu
asbury.to/firstfruits

BAPTISM:

MODE AND DESIGN.

BY

REV. W. B. GODBEY, A. M.

OF THE KENTUCKY CONFERENCE.

PENTECOSTAL PUBLISHING CO.,
Louisville, Ky.

PREFACE

Pursuant to the constant importunities of friends corroborated by conscientious convictions, I turn myself over to the Lord, permitting Him to use me for His glorification in the following elucidation of Christian baptism. We write not for theologians, but for the people. But as we have had so many debates on this subject, especially in Kentucky, let me here distinctly state, If any one desires to controvert this book, it will afford the author great pleasure to meet him at the time and place he may designate.

As this book is not for the learned, but for the people, I shall not encumber it with dead languages, but give in English the substance of vast and variant lingual, critical and historical data, for which I am personally responsible. I shall freely and frequently advert to the valuable and compendious works of Drs. Ditzler and Chapman, in which hundreds of authors are faithfully quoted.

ABBREVIATIONS.

V.——Verse.

H.——Hebrew Bible.

G.——Greek Bible.

L.——Latin Bible.

D.——Ditzler on Baptism.

C.——Chapman on Baptism.

i. e., id. est—that is. Figures refer to **pages.**

INTRODUCTORY.

As the Eucharist is the institution of Christ illustrating the atonement, equally significantly is baptism the ordinance of the Holy Ghost, the sanctifier and vitalizer of the world. The Holy Ghost is frequently illustrated by the falling rain upon the thirsty earth. Ps. lxxii: 6: "The (Holy Spirit) shall come down like rain. * * As showers that water the earth."

The rain is the water of temporal life. The Holy Spirit is the water of spiritual life. Without the former the world would become a desert uninhabited by man or beast ; without the latter it would become a hell inhabited only by devils incarnate and excarnate. So baptism with water is the beautiful emblem of spiritual life and purity.

The reason why we write these pages is because this beautiful and simple emblem by human device has been transformed into a hideous and monstrous water-god, an uncompromising rival of Jesus Christ.

We pray the Holy Spirit to use this little book as an iconoclast to destroy this idol, that the people may be saved.

In the following scriptures baptism is defined a symbolic purification, John iii: 25 ; Luke xi: 38 ; Titus iii: 5 ; Ezekiel xxxvi: 25 ; Isa lii : 15.

BAPTISM—MODE AND DESIGN.

PART I.

MODE.

The Bible mode is always affusion. The element is invariably administered to the subject. The plain and simple statement of the Bible everywhere precludes the probability of an immersion.

We believe an immersion will do for baptism, but that it was ever practiced by prophet or apostle we positively deny.

We find not a trace of immersion till the third century. Then it is mentioned in such a way as to preclude its apostolic practice. Immerse never occurs in the Bible, while sprinkle and pour occur frequently.

(C. 215). Tertullian early in the third century writes in reference to the trine naked immer-

sions of his day : "We immerse (L. mergo)
thrice, doing somewhat more than our Lord re-
quireth." The same author says : "John the
Baptist sprinkled (L. tingo), Peter sprinkled
(L. tingo) and Christ sent the apostles that
they should sprinkle (L. tingo) the nations."

Now remember, failing to find immerse in the
Bible, we go to history and here find it for the
first time.

Meanwhile the same author certifies John
sprinkled, Peter sprinkled and Christ sent the
apostles that they should sprinkle the nations.

I may here observe the singular fact that the
Immersionists in desperation, to rescue a sinking
cause from hopeless ruin, stoutly deny that
tingo ever means anything but immerse. In all
our definitions, please remember we admit (L.)
tingo,(G.) baptidzo and (H.) tabhal are words of
various meanings, among which are affuse, i. e.,
sprinkle, and pour, and immerse. A. Campbell
gives (G.) baptidzo twenty different meanings.
(D. 101). All we claim is that the Bible settles
its Bible meaning to be affusion.

That Tertullian uses (L.) tingo in the sense
of sprinkle is absolutely certain. Why would
he say we (L.) mergo (immerse) and John the
Baptist, Peter and the apostles (L.) tingo

(sprinkled) if mergo and tingo were synonymous? They are not synonymous ; for tingo means sprinkle, but immerse never. The following cases settle Tertullian's meaning to be sprinkle : Speaking of the heathens baptizing in imitation of the Christians. In the sacred rites of Isis, in the Apollinarian and Eleusinian rites, houses, temples and whole cities are baptized (L.) tingo. D. 284 and C. 270. Here and in other similar cases, there can be no cavil. They did not immerse these houses, temples and whole cities in water, yet Tertullian says they tingoed them, when we all know they sprinkled them. So Tertullian says John the Baptist, Peter and the apostles tingoed the people, *i. e.*, sprinkled them.

LEXICONS.

On (H.) tabhal,(G.) baptidzo and (L.) tingo, the words translated baptize.

Buxtorf, the Father of Hebrew lexicography, bearing date 1689, gives first definition (L.) tingo, used in Dan. iv: 12, to denote Nebuchadnezzar's sprinkling with dew; also v. 20 (L.) conspergo, to sprinkle and v. 22 (L.) infundo, to pour upon.

Dr. Furst, the prince of Hebrew scholars at the present day, defines the word (L.) **rigare,** tingere, to moisten, to sprinkle. The Hebrew is the primary authority and settles the controversy in favor of affusion. The following Greek Lexicons define baptidzo affuse. Julianus (L.) perfundere, to sprinkle. Stokius (L.) raino, perfundo, aspergo, sprinkle ; Ed. Leigh, Schleusner, Enthymius, Stephanus, Schrevelius, Grimshaw. Of these we would call especial attention to the definition of Schleusner, whose scholarship is acknowledged pre-eminent. We have his works in two large volumes elaborately defining every New Testament word.

Like many other authors he first gives immerse and then proceeds to state "in this definition, it never occurs in the New Testament, but in the sense of purgo (purify), abluo (wash), and lave (sprinkle), and metaphorically to pour forth largely "

Robinson gives a similar definition.

The Immersionists are forced by their dogma and practice to assume that (H.) tabhal, (G.) baptidzo and (L.) tingo always mean immerse and immerse only. Dr. Carson, the prince of Immersionists, well said : " In this I have all the lexicographers and commentators against me. "

Under this "onus probandi, " they are everywhere breaking down. Dr Conant has made the ablest effort in all the world and the ablest that ever will be made to sustain the dogma and signally and hopelessly failed. Many of his own examples, instead of establishing immersion, refute it; so he cuts his own head off a dozen times. His Baptizein, which is an utter and hopeless breakdown, is the last rally of the Immersionists.

Twenty-five years ago, they all wanted to affirm immersion. Now, we can seldom get them to deny affusion. At that time this book would have provoked a hundred challenges for debate; now, I fear, the battlefield will be silent.

HISTORY.

The Immersionists are always vociferating that Novatian, in A. D. 251, was the first case of affusion baptism. This is a great mistake. We trace affusion, in an unbroken succession, not only to the apostles, but to Moses.

Eusebius relates that when the Apostle John reclaimed a fallen disciple he was so penitent as to be baptized by flowing tears.

Walker relates that a Jew in the time of the apostles was baptized by pouring sand on him. (C. 101.)

Origen, the most learned man of his day, born only 85 years after the apostles, his father and grandfather being Christians—of course the latter contemporary with the apostles—comments on the transaction at Mt. Carmel (1 Kings xviii : 31–8), when Elijah poured water on the altar, and describes it by (G.) baptidzo; also certifying that John the Baptist did the same thing. So here is the most learned of all the fathers, his family contemporary with the apostles, himself a native Greek, using the New Tesment Greek word to denote the pouring of water on the altar and transferring the case at once to John the Baptist's pouring at the Jordan (Dale's Judaic Baptism, 328). Bishop Caslistus, A. D. 222, and St. Lawrence, A. D. 250, both baptized by affusion on the occasions of their own martyrdom (Martyrology of Ado, C. 34.)

The learned Lactantius, A. D. 320, states Christ would save the people by pouring on them the purifying water (C. 101.) Aurelius Prudentius and Bishop of Nola, A. D. 390, state that John poured the water on the people (C.234–5)⁻

St. Barnard states that John poured the water on the head of his Creator. (C. 138.)

The Waldenses have existed from the apostolic age. They baptize by affusion.

The Immersionists quote many historians certifying immersion; but please remember they are all modern men and quote no ancient author. Hence their testimony is null and void; amounting to no more than their own opinions.

No wonder the Immersionists quote no ancient men, for they all certify affusion.

Trine-naked immersion is first heard of in the third century with the incoming dark ages.

The single dip was first invented by Eunomius, A. D. 440 (Sozomon, D. 288 and C. 275.)

FIRST TESTIMONY.

Ezekiel xxxvi: 25: "I will sprinkle clean water upon you." And Isaiah lii: 15: "So shall he sprinkle many nations."

These prophets, inspired by the infallible Holy Ghost, contemplating all future ages in panoramic visions, till the world is dazzled with the splendors of the judgment throne, exultantly behold the triumphs of the gospel till every idol is dethroned and every idolater sprinkled with clear water, i. e., baptized into the church, and Christ enthroned in every heart. Meanwhile millennial glory will encircle the globe. These statements are unmistakable and irrefutable. We are forced to accept baptism by sprinkling or reject the Bible.

Could our immersion friends find a corresponding scripture in their favor, *i. e.*, "I will immerse you in water," how they would shout. They would write it over every church door. The artifice that would explain away these scriptures would take your Bible from you. So beware. Hold to your Bible and the question is settled in favor of sprinkling. These scriptures can't be evaded, from the fact that the church sprinkles water for nothing but baptism.

The scholars of all ages have interpreted these scriptures to mean baptism.

We could give the names of the brightest sages, from Origen, the father of commentators, down to the present, explaining this to be water baptism. But how can you deny it? You can't, if you will throw down your prejudice.

SECOND TESTIMONY.

Moses, (Ex. xv: 10;) David, (Psa. lxxvii: 17;) Paul, (1 Cor. x: 10 and Heb. ix: 10, 13, 19.) Moses certifies the Egyptians were immersed and the Israelites passed through dry-shod, *i. e.*, were not immersed; while Paul certifies that the Israelites were all baptized and David tells the mode, *i. e.*, "the clouds poured forth water." So Moses, David and Paul collaterally reveal the fact that the Israelites were baptized by sprink-

ling and not immersed. I am well acquainted
with the vast tergiversations resorted to by our
opponents to evade the unanswerable testimony
of these inspired witnesses to affusion, but they
are all in vain.

So, reader, whenever the Lord sends a shower
of rain from heaven, look at it and you will see
God's mode of baptism, by which he baptized
his people when they passed through the sea.
Under Judaism ceremonies were very operose;
baptism might be repeated indefinitely.

In Heb. ix: 10, Paul speaks of diaphorois bap-
tismois (G.) diverse baptisms—9th verse sprinkling—and 19th verse: " Moses sprinkled all the
people at the tabernacle door," i. e., baptized
all the people. . . So I find Moses was a great
Baptist, and an equally great sprinkler, since
he baptized three millions of people by sprinkling at the tabernacle door, as certified by Paul.

The Jews practiced baptism constantly—that
they sprinkled is clearly revealed : Lev. xiv: 7,
and Num. xix: 19.

That they ever immersed can't be proved by
the Bible.

THIRD TESTIMONY.

We now introduce John the Baptist on Jordan's bank. Did he immerse or affuse?

Against the probability of immersion we adduce its impossibility. Matth. iii : 5, 6, says he baptized the people of Jerusalem, all Judea, and all the regions round about Jordan, *i. e.*, six millions of people. He was only engaged six months. The calculation, allowing ten hours per day, would require him to baptize sixty persons per minute. Besides, the Jordan is very cold and flows with the impetuosity of a mountain torrent. (D. 41.) Standing in the cold water would arrest circulation and quickly produce paralysis and death.

One-fourth of the number certified by Matthew would equal the entire population of Kentucky. Where is the man who could immerse all the people of Kentucky in the beautiful and placid Ohio? That man don't live. An antediluvian giant would wear out and die before he laid all the people of Kentucky on their backs in the river and lifted them out by physical power. Did John in six months immerse four times that number? You can't believe it if you try. Especially when John tells you the very opposite; for he says he handled the water and not the people, always using hudati (G.) with water, in the instrumental dative.

The regular New Testament construction, hudati (G.), precludes the possibility of immersion. "Motion to governs the accusative" is a fundamental rule of Greek grammar. Pursuant to this invariable rule of the Greek language, if they had immersed we would invariably have "baptidzo eis to hudor" (G.), the accusative case governed by eis (G.), instead of "en to hudati (G.), or as it often occurs with stronger force without a preposition, simply hudati (G.) (Mark i: 8; Luke iii: 16; Acts i: 5; xi: 16; Heb. x: 22.) The doctrine of instrumentality without a preposition, showing beyond the possibility of cavil that the water was handled and applied to the people, and not the people handled and applied to the water. This position is corroborated by every passage in the Bible.

In addition to the baptism of the New Testament we cite from the Septuagint:

1 Kings xviii: 3: Obediah fed the prophets with bread and water, "hudati" (G.); Neh. xiii: 2: Amonites and Moabites met not Israel with bread and water, "hudati" (G.)

Ezek. xvi: 4: "Thou wast not washed in with water, "hudati" (G.) 9th verse: I washed thee with water, "hudati" (G.); Num. xix: 19,

in water, "hudati," (G.); 2 Kings viii: 15:
"Hazael (bapto, G.) wet the cloth with water,
"hudati" (G.)

On the contrary, we find when the person or
thing falls (as in case of immersion) into the
water, we invariably have the accusative with
eis. Matth. xvii: 15: Falls into the water
(eis to hudor, G.) (Latin immerse). Acts vii:
24: "Often causeth him to fall into the water"
(eis hudata, G.) 2 Kings vi: 5: "Ax fell
into the water" (eis to hudor, G.)

Ex. xv: 25: "Moses fell a tree into the
water" (eis to hudor, G.)

Josh. iii. 15: "The priests dipped their feet
into the brim of water."

So every Bible case of immersion (there is
none for Baptism by immersion) takes water in
the accusative; whereas in every case of baptism it is in the dative. Hence the idea of immersion is incompatible with the grammatical
construction of the Greek Testament.

I used this argument in debate with Elder
Briney (one of the ablest immersionists in the
world), at Little Hickman, May 1st, 1883. His
only attempted refutation was a reference to
Mark i: 9, ("eis ton Iordaneen, G.), which is not
a parallel case, being the accusative of place as

(Acts 8 : 38) at Azotus, and (Matth. v : 35) by
Jerusalem. But never did he even attempt to
meet the argument. If John had immersed
those people he would have said, "baptidzo
humas eis to hudor" (G.), whereas he said,
(Matth. iii : 11) baptidzo humas en hudati
(G.), positively revealing the fact that he applied the water to the people, instead of apply-
ing the people to the water, which is really
the case in immersion.

It is an indisputable fact that immersion never
can be harmonized with the Greek Testament.
The construction requires affusion and precludes
immersion.

Again : John tells us he poured the water on
the people at the Jordan. He says: "I baptize
you with water, and Jesus will baptize you with
the Holy Ghost." So he uses the same word to
reveal what he does to the people with water
and what Jesus does with the Holy Ghost;
hence it is a matter of positive and unmistakable revelation that John and Jesus did the
same thing, and that thing is revealed by the
word baptize. If John had not done the same
thing with water that Jesus did with Spirit and
fire he would not have used the same word to
tell what he did, and also what Jesus did. Then

what did John and Jesus do?—for the Bible
says they did the same thing—the difference
not in what they did, but the element used;
namely, water in one case and Spirit and fire in
the other. But fortunately the Bible reveals
in many places (Acts i: 8; ii: 17, 18; x: 44)
that Jesus poured when he baptized. Don't
you know that is equivalent to saying John
poured when he baptized?

If the people were in the Jordan waist deep
it don't modify the case. John poured the water
on them, for he says he did. You know Jesus
poured and can't deny it. Then how can you
say John immersed, i. e, did the very opposite,
when the same word tells what both admin-
istrators did? If John immersed, Jesus immersed; but you know the Bible everywhere
says he poured.. If John plunged the people into
the water, Jesus plunged them into the Holy
Ghost and fire; but the Bible says the Spirit
fell on them and the fire fell on them Then
we are inevasibly driven to the conclusion that
the water fell on them. Jesus poured the Spirit
and fire on them, and it is equally certain John
poured the water on them.

The Greek Scripture gives us no evidence that
John and his people were in the water. It don't

say they went in, and the statement "came out" is well known to be a wrong translation, and is corrected in the revised version of 1881, and reads "came up from" the water, only implying that he was at it and not in it. The expression "in Jordan," is perfectly correctly translated "at Jordan," or "on Jordan;" just as we would say on the Ohio

We have not the slightest assurance that any of the baptismal parties spoken of in the New Testament were ever in the water. Out of the fourteen recorded baptisms only three of them were at the water. They were generally in houses But suppose they baptized in rivers; it is equally clear they poured, for the Bible everywhere says so.

Moses baptized all the people by sprinkling as they stood at the tabernacle door (Heb ix : 10, 19). The Jewish priests, from the days of Moses, had baptized by sprinkling. John was born a priest. He uses the same word to denote his administrations used by Paul (Heb. ix : 10), to denote the sprinkling. So how can we conclude he changed the ordinance?

As Moses stood at the tabernacle door and sprinkled the people standing round him, so we conclude John stood on Jordan's bank, dipped the hyssop in the water and sprinkled the multitudes. So all the ancient statuary represent our Savior standing and John pouring water on his head. Some of these statues date within about one hundred years of the apostles. Thus we have the unanimous (C. 125) testimony of all history and all Scripture that John baptized by affusion.

FOURTH TESTIMONY—PENTECOST,

in which Jesus, Paul, Peter, Luke and John the Baptist commingle their familiar voices.

Here are facts accompanied by incontestable demonstrations. Jesus commanded his apostles to go and baptize every person in the whole world; *i. e.*, to do something to everybody which he revealed by the word "baptize." Now, lest they should be mistaken in reference to what they are to do, he positively forbids them to begin till he does the same thing to them which they are to do to all the people in the world. The only difference is he uses spirit and fire, and they are to use water, because the same word "baptize" tells what both Jesus and his apostles are to do.

Now, what is it?

The auspicious day comes   Jesus pours out his spirit on them (Acts ii: 17, 18).   The Holy

Spirit came upon them (Acts i : 8), and the fire
sat on them (Acts ii : 3). The same day 3,000
were baptized with water, and in a few hours
5,000 more. How was it done? It is revealed
above —the water fell on them. Jesus gave them
an illustrative example and they followed it.
He poured and they poured.

Hence, there in that mountain city, distin-
guished in all ages for its scarcity of water in
the dry season (and this was in June), and supplied at that time by the pools of Solomon, twelve
miles distant in the mountains—there is no
difficulty in baptizing the 3,000 during the fore-
noon services; and they entered upon the afternoon service at 3 o'clock (Acts iii : 1).

This expedition is irreconcilable with immersion, and abundantly corroborates the Scripture
statement that it was affusion. Now, reader,
please remember Pentecost is no longer a day,
but a dispensation—the brightest and the best,
the full-orbed gospel in splendor and glory un-
precedented since the world began, while you
and I are so fortunate as to live amid this grand
pentecostal light and glory.

John the Baptist having preached the gospel
prologue, and baptized with water, introduced
Jesus, the Great Baptizer, and retired. Has

Jesus baptized you? Don't wait. If he don't baptize you with the Holy Ghost and fire, there is no room for you in heaven. Jesus is the only Baptizer; we symbolize with water, but Jesus does the baptizing. How can you believe the pentecostal preachers plunged when the Bible states positively that Jesus poured, and the preachers did the same thing with water?

If you will read that Scripture and let it mean what it says, you *can't* believe they were immersed unless you take the position of a giant immersionist, in debate with me, "that they were immersed by pouring!!!" I responded: "Quantity is not in question. If you pour the Atlantic Ocean on a man, he is baptized by pouring."

One of my great objections to immersion is that it ignores and detracts attention from our Savior's baptism, without which all water baptisms are farcical, nonsensical and blasphemous. At Pentecost the two baptisms are in so close proximity, and the mode revealed in so plain phraseology, "poured out" and "fell on them," that nothing but sectarian prejudice could ever so much as raise a quibble in the mind of the reader. I have often debated with iron-bound sectarians who, in desperation, would leap to the suicidal ultimatum of denying that there is any such a thing as Holy Ghost baptism. They quote Paul to (Eph. i : 5) "one baptism." To this we reply that Paul is there expounding the economy of grace, in which there is but one baptism, namely, that of the spirit.

But the same apostle, in Heb. vi : 2, describing the gospel rudiments, speaks of "baptisms"—at least two, namely, that of water and that of the Spirit.

Aside from the fact that the Bible abounds in Holy Ghost baptisms, and there is no salvation without it—for out of Christ there is no salvation, and no one can get into him but by the baptism of the Holy Ghost (Rom. vi : 3, Gal. iii : 27, and 1 Cor. xii : 13)—Peter promptly settles the question forever (Acts ii : 39) in his pentecostal sermon: "So the promise is made unto you and to your children, and to all who are afar off, even as many as the Lord our God shall call."

The "promise" of what? Why, the baptism of the Holy Ghost, which came down and saved 3,000, and is still coming down and will continue to come down as long as fervent prayers go up. This is the only hope of the world; the only power that ever saved a soul or ever will. To deny the present and perpetual efficiency of

Holy Ghost baptism is the very doctrine of anti-christ. It dethrones Jesus and enthrones the water god.

And for what are all these suicidal lunges? Why, to save immersion, an institution unknown in the Bible, and never once he rd of till after every inspired man had gone to heaven. If you would see the falsity of a doctrine, you have nothing to do but follow it into its labyrinthine absurdities. Here we see men of learning and intelligence throwing away the only real and substantial baptism, on which depends the salvation of their souls, and all for what? Why, to get rid of the Bible mode and sustain a sectarian cause

FIFTH TESTIMONY.

Philip (Acts viii: 38, Isaiah lii: 15): " So shall he sprinkle many nations. " (And Matth. xvii: 27.)

Here Philip falls in with the Ethiopian eunuch, preaches the gospel to him, and baptizes him. He takes for his text the messianic prophecies of Isaiah, which the eunuch was reading, and as he baptized him we conclude he preached baptism. The only baptism in his text was by sprinkling. So we are forced to conclude that he sprinkled him. But, you say, he went into

the water. Then what did he do? His text
says "sprinkle." So I conclude he sprinkled
him.

His text from the evangelical prophet had
nothing but "sprinkle," but Luke says that he
baptized him. Then how shall I understand
Luke? The Bible is a self-interpreter. Hence
my only appeal is to the Bible itself. That the
solution may be close, clear and conclusive, I
take the same author (Luke) and let him explain himself. He tells in Acts i: 2, that Jesus
did the same thing to his apostles at Pentecost,
with the Holy Ghost and fire, that Philip did
to the eunuch with water, but he tells me Jesus
poured the Spirit on them. So I have the Bible
answer Philip poured the water on the eunuch.
(Sprinkle and pour are both affusion and the
same.) Bloomfield (D. 348), Jameson, Fauset,
Brown, Olshausen and Baumgarten (D. 354), the
great lights of exegesis, corroborate this interpretation. While the Bible settles the question
that the eunuch was baptized by affusion, the
inquiry is raised, why did they go into the
water? This don't concern the matter in dis-
pute, because the going in and coming out were
not the baptism, and the case is as clear that it
was an affusion, if they waded in as if they

stopped at the edge. But we would gratuit-
ously here observe, there is no assurance in the
original that they either went in or came out.
The Greek is fully satisfied by the translation.
They went down (down here means out of the
chariot and is antithetical to "up" in verse 31) to
the water and came up from the water. (G.) eis
has about twenty meanings, and no one more
prominent than to. In Matth. xvii: 27, we
have the same statement in Greek in reference
to Peter going down to the sea to catch a fish
with hook and line. You don't believe Peter
waded into the sea to catch the fish; then you
need not believe Philip and the eunuch waded
into the water for the baptism

In Gen. 28: 16, we have the same Greek
compounds, "Katabe and anabe," with reference
to Rebecca going to the fountain, but there
was no entrance.

In Tobit vi: 3, we have it again, in reference
to a young man going down to the river, but
there was no entrance.

The Spring Bethsoron, at which Philip baptized the Ethiopian eunuch, was well known in
the fourth century, as related by Eusebius.

SIXTH TESTIMONY,

By Peter and Luke at the house of Cornelius.

Peter is preaching to a spell-bound audience, powerfully wrought upon by the contrition and piety of Cornelius, now with thrilling enthusiasm listening to their first gospel sermon. He reaches the climax and tells them precisely how to be saved, proving his doctrine by all the prophets (Acts x: 43): "To him give all the prophets witness, that through his name whosoever believeth in him shall receive remission of sins." This is the golden key with which they unlock the kingdom of heaven. Now, pursuant to God's great law, faith in Christ, they are pardoned, and Jesus sets his seal upon it, baptizing them with the Holy Ghost. They break forth into a jubilant halleluiah, and shout the preacher down.

Now what is the revelation on the mode of baptism? It is clear as the meridian sun. Jesus baptizes Peter's congregation while he is preaching to them; and what was the mode? Acts x: 44: "The Holy Ghost fell on them." When Peter saw his Savior had baptized his congregation he immediately said he would do the same thing with water. And so the inspired historian Luke says he did it. Remember Peter uses the same word baptize to describe what he did with water and what Jesus did with the

Holy Ghost. So we are coerced to conclude he
did the same thing. If he had not done the
same thing he would have used a different word
to describe what he did. But Peter says he did
the same thing with water that Jesus did with
the Holy Ghost. But the Holy Ghost fell on
them. So Peter says the water fell on them
If Peter had plunged could he have revealed
his plunging and Jesus' pouring by the same
word? "Fell on them" verse 44, reveals the
mode of baptism both by Spirit and water.

The whole narrative shows they were baptized by affusion there in the house.

(G.) "To hudor kolusai,' verse 47, reveals
the fact that the water was moved to the people
instead of the people to the water.

SEVENTH TESTIMONY,

By Paul and Luke (Acts xvi: 33)—Jailor.
Pursuant to the heavenly vision Paul has bidden
adieu to his native Asia and come to Europe to
preach the gospel; has arrived at Philippi, the
Roman metropolis. Upon his ejection of a
familiar spirit from a damsel he and Silas are
arrested, arraigned and condemned. The stout
Roman lictors lacerate their naked backs with
the cruel rods, sending every stroke to the bone.
They are committed to the merciless heathen

jailor for safe keeping. He leads them down
into the dismal dreary dungeon and lays their
bleeding backs on the cold stone floor, lifts up
their feet, fastens them in the cruel stocks, goes
back to his downy bed and lies down to take his
rest.

Meanwhile Paul says to Silas: "O my son,
how sweet it is to suffer for Jesus, who died for
us? Would it not be glorious if we would get
to die for him?" Says Silas: "I was so happy
all the time they were beating us. I saw heaven
open, while glory filled my soul."

They then pray for that wicked city, and
especially for the cruel jailor.

Jesus comes to see them. Their souls get
happy They sing praises to God and the Lamb.
They shout glory. Then power comes down.
God answers them with an earthquake. The
old prison rocks to and fro. The bars and bolts
are all snapped. The ponderous iron doors slam
back against the massive stone walls like claps
of thunder. The prisoners are loose. Paul
looks through the open door into the jailor's
apartment (in the same building), and sees him
draw the sword to cut his throat; thinking the
prisoners had escaped and his life would pay
the forfeiture, prefers suicide. The earthquake,

accompanied by the startling information, "We are all here," convicts him so pungently, he falls and cries, "What shall I do to be saved?" The gospel answer comes promptly, "Believe on the Lord Jesus Christ and thou shalt be saved." He believes, is converted, and goes shouting round over the house, happy in the Lord. At the same hour (midnight) he washed their stripes and was baptized. Did they go out to hunt immersion water? They did not. There is but one "out" in the text, and that took them out of the dungeon into the hall.

Again : Paul's veracity assures us he did not go out of that jail till after the baptism. When the sergeants came and told him to go, he said, "Nay, verily." Then the magistrates came and brought them out. So, if we respect Paul's veracity, we dare not say he had been out of that jail.

John Wesley, D. 350 ; Witseus. D. 352 ; Baumgarten, D 347, and Moses Stuart, D. 356, men at whose feet we all delight to sit, give it as their opinion that Paul took from the same water brought into the house to "wash their stripes," and baptized the jailor, wife and little ones.

Besides, let us bear in mind that the modal

signification of baptism throughout the Bible is affusion.

EIGHTH TESTIMONY,

By Ananias (Acts xxii. 16)—the baptism of Saul. Here is a weeping penitent, lacerated with contrition, having spent three days and nights in awful agony, neither eating nor sleeping. Ananias preaches to him, exhorts him and prays for him. The "scales fall from his eyes," his soul is converted. The preacher says arise, (G.) anastas, "standing up," be baptized. Now we have it all. The man gets up and is baptized, and unless you manufacture scripture you can't get him out of his tracks, not to say out of the house and going off to hunt an immersion pool.

NINTH TESTIMONY,

Our Lord's commission (Matth. xxviii: 19.) Our Savior commands us to baptize all the people in the world. He commands nothing impossible or unreasonable.

We can baptize everybody, but we can't immerse everybody.

We are commanded to baptize the eight millions of people living around the North pole. To immerse them would kill both the subject and administrator. Millions of people amid

sandy deserts can be baptized, but can't be immersed.

I was well acquainted with two Baptist
preachers in Pulaski County, Ky., who immersed people in Pitman's Creek when the water
was cold, went home, took their beds and soon
left them for their graves.

When presiding elder in southeastern Kentucky, on arrival at Meadow Creek, Whitley
County, to hold my quarterly meeting, I was
informed of a sudden death a day or two ago.
A man low with consumption desired immersion.
During an attempt made by his friends to sub-
merge him in a canoe, before he had sunk beneath the waves of cold Cumberland, the shock
was so great, the blood rushed so violently to
the interior as to rupture the vessels and produce frightful hemorrhage from the nose and
mouth. He was instantly lifted out dead.

A young man was immersed in Salt River,
Kentucky, a few years ago, and fell dead on the
bank.

A man was put into water for immersion
near St Joseph, Mo , and taken out dead.

Cases can be given indefinitely

Jesus said he "came not to destroy men's
lives, but to save them."

Immersion destroys life.   Hence it is not the institution of Jesus.

TENTH TESTIMONY.

The apostolic persecutions prove that they did not immerse the people.

Now, reader, just take into consideration the fact that the apostles penetrated the heathen nations and labored faithfully till bloody death gave them a sweet passport to glory.   They were all persecuted unto death except John, who was miraculously delivered from the caldron of boiling oil in Rome.

Now remember the Christian religion was utterly new to the heathens in every respect.

Now suppose you had never seen nor heard of baptism.   A band of strangers come to your village preaching and immersing the people. Don't you know, when they would lead the candidates down into the river and proceed to immerse them, it would look just like they were going to drown them?   Don't you know, if the apostles had immersed the mob would have assaulted them?   If Paul, at Philippi, had undertaken to immerse Lydia in that river on whose bank she was converted, her friends would have rallied and flogged him more terribly than they ever did for preaching.   I have

2

my doubts whether he would have gotten out of that river without a broken head.

Here is the clear fact; the heathens who persecuted them even unto death for preaching, would have persecuted them for immersion. The very fact that they never were persecuted for it is positive proof they never did it. All analogy involves the conclusion they never would have permitted them to immerse their women. They would have persecuted them much more for immersion than for preaching.

The very fact that they never persecuted them on account of their baptisms is unanswerable negative proof that their baptisms were not immersions, but simple affusions, so unostensible as to be passed over unnoticed by their enemies.

ELEVENTH TESTIMONY.

Mark vii: 4; Luke xi: 38. In these scriptures, where you have "wash" in English we have baptize in Greek. In the fourth verse we have this wash twice in English; in one of these the Greek baptismous, baptisms; in the other (G.)"rantisoontai," the regular word for sprinkle, clearly illustrating the synonymy of baptize and sprinkle, because Mark uses (G.) "rantisoontai" (sprinkle.) interchangeably with "bap-

tisoontai" (baptize.)   See Critical Greek Testa·
ment by Hort and Westcott, 1881, latest decision
of all the critics and highest New Testament
authority in the world.

You see it settles this question forever by defining (G.) "baptidzo" (baptize) by (G) ran-
tidzo" (sprinkle.)

TWELFTH TESTIMONY.

The Latin Bible.

We find immersion nowhere in the English
Bible; but since it is a Latin word, we go to the
Latin Bible and find it in many passages. The
Latin Bible (Itala) was translated early in the
second century by the disciples of the apostles,
and revised in fourth century by the learned
Jerome.

Now remember this Bible was made by the
holy men who had seen the apostles baptize the
people.

Did the apostles immerse? Would they not
have said so? I go to this Bible and find immerse used whenever there was a sinking (for
sink is the meaning of immerse, as it don't mean
to take them out at all), as (Ex. xv: 10), "The
Egyptians sank" (were immersed). Jer. li: 64:
"Babylon will sink," i. e. (immerse). Matth.
xiv: 30: "Peter began to sink" (immerse).

Matth. xviii: 6: "Drowned in the depths of
the sea." Luke v: 7: "They began to sink"
(immerse). 1 Tim. vi: 9: "Which drown men
in destruction and perdition" (immerse).

When a man is immersed for baptism it is
just such an operation as the above. Then
why don't we find (L.) 'mergo" (immerse) in
the Latin Bible to denote baptism? There can
be but one answer to this question. That answer
is, "*Because the apostolic baptisms were not immersions.*" Thus you see the Latin Bible, in
which immerse is vernacular, sweeps away the
last possible presumption that there ever was an
immersion seen or heard of till after the apostles
had gone to heaven.

I can't see how a man can read the Latin
Bible and entertain the smallest conception that
immersion was ever seen till down the post-
apostolic ages human invention foisted it upon
the church.

I have given you twelve elaborate arguments
from Bible cases of water baptism, and find them
all affusions, without a trace or a track of immersion. My argument on Mode is at an end,
having taken indescrimately all the prominent
water baptisms.

You will be a little surprised when I tell you

I was baptized by immersion when about sixteen; educated in an immersion college, and started out preaching an honest immersionist. Why the change? One word tells it: Light, light, light! Glory be to God for light. Glory to his name for the baptism Jesus pours on my soul!

Reader, has Jesus baptized you? If not hasten to fall at his feet, and take him for your portion and receive his baptism, without which you will never dwell in his presence

ROMANS VI.

The reason why I proceed to expound this scripture is because, though it is spiritual baptism, since the beginning of the dark ages in the third century and the rise of trine-naked immersion, it has been the standing proof-text of immersionists. All other texts which have been used signally fail to furnish a solitary item of proof. All they can get out of other scriptures is merely local or circumstantial —such as being at the Jordan, or at Enon, where many springs flow, or even "in Jordan," proves nothing about the mode, and when we go to the Bible we find it was affusion, whether in a river or in a house. So it is an indisputable fact that the only arguments for immersion are the heathen literature,

the dark age practice of a fallen, idolatrous
church, and a false interpretation of Romans vi.
The falsity of the interpretation consists in its
application to water baptism. All I have to do
to refute the immersion argument is to prove
the pure spirituality of the passage.

The transaction in question embraces the first
eleven verses of the chapter. Let us examine
them in order and see whether they are physical
or spiritual.

Verse 2 : "Dead to sin " Is the body dead to
sin or the soul? You know it is the latter.
Verse 3 : "Were baptized into Jesus Christ?"
Is your body baptized into Jesus Christ? The
very idea is materialistic, idolatrous and blasphemous.

Verse 4: "Buried with him by baptism into
death." Is your body buried with the body
of Christ? You know it is not. Hence it is a
spiritual burial.

Verse 5 : "Planted together," (G.) "sum-
phutoi," grown together; from (G.) "sumphuoo,"
mistaken by James' translators to be from (G.)
"sumphuteuoo," planted together, and hence
erroneously translated "planted together," instead
of grown together.

The Bible represents every Christian as a

branch "cut out of the wild olive tree (Satan) Rom. xi., and "grafted into the good olive tree (Christ), and grown fast to him as the branch in the vine (John xv.) So our salvation depends on our being grafted into Christ and growing together with him.

Now we settle the question at once. Is this physical or spiritual? If it is physical, your body, Christian reader, is grown together with the body of Christ. But you know this is not so. The body of Christ was in heaven before your body had an existence. But it is a fact that your spirit in regeneration was grafted into the spiritual body of Christ and has grown fast to it and lives by virtue of the vitality derived from it. This one verse triumphantly refutes the possibility of a physical transaction.

Verse 6: "Old man crucified, . . destroyed." Is the "old man" your body? Is your body crucified and "destroyed" in water baptism? You know it is not.

How preposterous the application! The "old man" is your fallen nature, which is "crucified" and "destroyed" by the Holy Ghost in regeneration and sanctification.

Verse 7: "He that is dead is freed from sin." Is that physical? Then whenever a man is converted his body dies.

Verse 11: "Reckon yourselves dead unto sin." Is that your body? Then Christianity is for the dead and not for the living; for a man can never be a Christian while his body lives. So you see the utter falsity of the physical interpretation.

Water baptism is for the physical man. Hence it can't be water baptism. This is the most elaborate, clear and beautiful description of sanctification in the Bible. It is a great pity to have this scripture so perverted by immersionists. It is no more applicable to a man's body than to his horse. You are an immortal spirit. You, not your body, must follow Christ in crucifixion, interment and resurrection.

The "old man, *i. e.*, your fallen nature, must be crucified, *i. e.*, killed, "buried into death," *i. e.*, into the atonement, *i. e.*, washed away by his blood, *i. e.*, utterly "destroyed."

Thus the old nature is absolutely destroyed and taken away, and the new nature created by the supernatural intervention of the Holy Ghost, is raised up to walk in newness of life. Then all sin, actual and inbred (old man) is washed away, the heart is cleansed, and Christ reigns without a rival.

It is to be deplored that the immersion dogma

throws a dark shadow over this pre-eminently important scripture, deceives the people and keeps them from seeking the experience here described, without which they never can enter heaven. The baptism is not represented here as a burial, but as the burier, *i. e.*, "buried by baptism." Baptism is the agent of crucifixion, burial and resurrection.

The "old man," *i. e.*, inbred depravity, is crucified and buried into the death of Christ, *i. e.*, washed away by his blood, and the new man raised up, all by the baptism of the Holy Ghost. Burial is not the baptism, but one of the important spiritual effects of the baptism of the Holy Spirit. I here arraign my immersion brethren for contradicting St. Paul in the following points:

First. When you immerse a man you bury him alive, whereas Paul's man in burial is crucified, *i. e.*, dead, before he is buried. Now tell me by what authority you bury a man alive. You respond, O! his body is not dead, but his spirit. Then let us have a spiritual burial, and we all agree. The thing buried is dead. So if you bury the body you must wait till it is dead. But you bury them all alive. So you flatly contradict Paul. I arraign you for contradicting

Paul and disobeying the Scripture wherever you bury anything alive.

Second. Antagonism: You bury the man into water, whereas, the "old man" in the text is buried into "death" (of Christ), *i. e*, the fountain filled with blood where all our sins are washed away.

Third. Antagonism: You raise up the same body you bury, whereas, in the text the "old man," the son of the devil, is buried and left buried forever, *i. e.*, utterly "destroyed," washed away by the blood, leaving the soul "sanctified wholly," 1 Thess. v: 23, and the new man, the son of God, is raised up. If the ' old man" is raised up, "the last state of the man is worse than the first."

Fourth. Antagonism: You raise the man by your own physical power, whereas the man in the text is raised "through faith of the operation of God," *i. e.*, by the power of God through faith, *i. e.*, the crucifixion, interment and resurrection are all, like everything else we get from God, simply through faith.

So you see Rom. vi. is absolutely irreconcilable with the immersion. When you immerse a man you antagonize the Apostle Paul throughout. I would insist that you cease to mar that

glorious description of entire sanctification, *i. e.*,
full salvation, without the experience of which
your people will all go to hell. When you immerse people do like I do, immerse them for ac-
commodation, because I believe it will *do* for
baptism, and don't pervert and destroy the force
of God's word in the vain attempt to prove
something which is entirely unknown in the
Bible. Every word in the chapter (Rom. vi.)
proves the baptism to be spiritual. So you all
know the mode before I tell you. From the
alpha of Genesis to the omega of Revelation,
the Spirit is poured out on the people. The
effect of the baptism is to crucify the "old man,"
bury him into the atonement of Christ, and raise
up the "new man."

Reader, have you this experience? Has the
Holy Ghost crucified, buried and raised you?
If not, pray to Jesus this moment, linger at His
feet, plunge into the fountain. His blood will
wash away the "old man" and make you "whiter
than snow," Psa. li: 7.

Heb. x: 22, "Let us draw nigh with a true
heart, . . . and our bodies washed with
pure water." Immersion has often been in-
ferred from this, because it says "bodies washed."
There is no evidence that the entire body is

washed When Jesus said to Peter, John xiii: 8,
"If I wash thee not," *i. e.*, Peter, the man; he
only meant his feet.

Luke xi: 38, "They marveled that he had
not first washed before dinner," (G.) baptidzo,
whereas, they only meant wash his hands (Dr.
Wall, D. 354) From these and many other
scriptures we see the presumption that it means
the entire body is wholly untenable.

Again, the revelation of the Holy Spirit settles the question that no immersion can be in-
volved. "With pure water," in the Greek is
"hudati Katharoo." Katharoo is the word always involving the idea of sprinkling. It is
used in (Ezekiel xxxvi: 25), "I will sprinkle
clean water upon you." It means the water of
purification or baptism, which was always sprinkled.

"Hudati" (with water) is the dative without a
preposition, and is irreconcilable with an immersion. In fact, the Greek construction of this
passage precludes the possibility of an immersion. An immersion would require the accusative with a preposition; (G.) eis to hudor, into
the water; whereas, the text reads simply (G.)
"hudati," with water, showing that the water
was handled. I don't wonder that the light of

Christian civilization has almost driven immersion from the earth.

During the dark ages 500 years ago, it was prevalent throughout Europe; now it is almost unknown. Of the four hundred millions of nominal Christians to-day, only about four millions require immersion for baptism. Many of the Baptists, its strong defenders, having given it up, practice pouring. (Milner 162.)

Thus an institution, born of superstition, culminating in the dark ages, is fast waning and dying amid the accumulating light of growing civilization. It can't bear the light. It can't bear investigation We have had many debates in the Kentucky Conference, where this dogma is stronger than in any other territory of equal area beneath the skies But how is it now? The battlefield is silent. Only now and then we hear the clash of resounding arms.

PART II.

DESIGN.

Ezekiel xxxvi: 25, "I will sprinkle clean water upon you." . . . . A new heart will I give you, and a new spirit will I put within you."

John the Baptist, Matt. iii: 11, "I baptize you with water, but He (Jesus) will baptize you with the Holy Ghost and fire." These authors exhibit the uniform teaching of both testaments, setting forth both baptisms in the same sentence in immediate juxtaposition, illustrating mutual counterparts of the same transaction—namely, spiritual substance and ceremonial symbol, *i. e.*, water is the symbol of the Spirit.

I write not so much to establish the design of water baptism, which is very simple and all told in the mere symbol of Spirit, but to refute a monstrous heresy which has spread over this country during the last half century, namely baptismal remission. This, with other kindred

heresies, is the mystery of iniquity, 2 Th. ii: 7,
and the antichrist of prophecy.

2 Th. ii : 3, "And that man of sin be revealed,
the son of perdition; who opposeth and exalteth
himself above all that is called God, or that is
worshipped; so that he, as God, sitteth in the
temple of God, shewing himself that he is God."
In the debate at Little Hickman, Jessamine
County, Ky., May 1-4, 1883, Elder Briney
argued that when God converted a man, still he
was not pardoned till he was immersed for the
remission of his sins. You see this is a full in-
dorsement of popery, elevating the Pope or the
preacher above God. For after God has converted the man, he must still go to hell, unless
the preacher immerses him. So Jesus don't
save him in conversion, but the preacher saves
him in immersion. The heathens all believed in
the efficacy of water to wash away spiritual
pollutions, (D. 284).

When the heathens came by myriads into the
church, they brought with them this doctrine,
which became the pillar of popery, prelacy
and priestcraft. The result of this influx of
heathen heresy was the paganization of the
church and its transformation from the sim-
plicity of Apostolic doctrine and practice into

the hideous monstrosity of Roman Catholicism. During the dark ages the Romanists immersed for remission. With the incoming light of modern civilization they gave up their unscrip- tural immersion, and have since sprinkled for remission.

Sixty years ago Elder A. Campbell, a man of erudition and eloquence, began to propagate his new doctrine in this country "immersion for re- mission." The people flocked from all direc- tions, listened spellbound and followed him by myriads. Little did they apprehend that the new doctrine they were drinking in so voraci- ously was "dark age popery," exhumed by this ingenious son of thunder.

A man would a thousand times better never receive water baptism than to receive it as a sav- ing ordinance, for in that case it becomes a rival of Jesus. You worship everything to which you impute salvation. If you look to baptism as a saving ordinance in any sense, you deify it and become an idolater. If you go to the water imbued with this heresy, that God has promised to remit your sins in water baptism, you come away unpardoned, and so remain until you aban- don the water-god and take Jesus. The only condition on which Jesus will save, is to abandon everything, *i. e.*, the water, the preacher and everything else, and take Him alone and trust Him to save you.

OBEDIENCE.

The advocates of this specious and dangerous error talk much about obedience. St. James ii: 10, "Whosoever . . . offends the law in one point, is guilty of all, plainly teaches the unity of disobedience. Disobedience is but the antithesis of obedience. If one is a unit, so is the other.

That unit of obedience Jesus has revealed by *one* word, *love.* "Thou shalt love the Lord with all thy heart." . . . Again, "Love is the fulfilling of the law" (Rom. xiii: 10).

SALVATION.

In the salvation of a soul, there are conviction, repentance, faith, justification, regeneration, adoption, baptism and obedience. Conviction shows us we are lost; repentance breaks the yoke of Satan and abandons him forever; faith receives Christ and submits to Him unconditionally. Christ baptizes us with his Holy Spirit, who sheds abroad (pours out) his love in our hearts, Rom. v: 5. This love regenerates you, the Spirit adopts you and testifies to you your salvation.

Rom. v: 5, tells you how you get the love.
It is "poured into" your heart by the Holy
Ghost. Now, Jesus settles the question of obedience by concentrating all the commandments
into one, and that is "love," Math. xxii : 37,
and Paul confirms it—"*Love*" is the fulfilling of
the law.

The moment a sinner abandons himself to
Christ, He forgives his sins, baptizes his soul
and pours into his heart His love, which is the
essence of all obedience.

Away with your popes and priests! We can
only tell the sinners about Jesus and send them
to him. He needs no help to save them, and
won't have any. When you and the water-God
pitch in to help Him, he modestly declines and
leaves you the job by yourselves, and will never
save unless the sinner gets his eyes open, sees
you and the water-God can't save him, and in
despair turns himself over to Jesus. You see I
have proved that the love Jesus gives you when
He converts you is the only obedience. That
love which is the inward and only essential
obedience of course leads a life of outward obedience also. But the outward obedience, whether
in water baptism or ten thousand other duties
equally important, is but the fruit of the only

real and essential obedience, that blessed heavenly unit, an artesian well of holy love ever flowing
in the soul, without which all outward obedience as a condition of salvation, is idolatrous,
papistical, nonsensical and blasphemous.

ANTICHRIST.

A moment's reflection in the light of God's
word will enable you to see that this is the doc-
trince of antichrist.

Antichrist is one who usurps the throne of
Christ, *i. e.*, takes the place of Christ and keeps
Christ from saving the peeple.

Jesus is the omnipotent King of the universe.
The very idea that He needs help to save a soul
is idolatrous, blasphemous and downright insult
to His majesty.

You can easily discriminate between the
preacher of Christ and the preacher of antichrist. The former cries : "Fly to Christ and
let Him save you; " the latter, whether Mormon prophet or Roman priest, vociferates,
"Come to *me*, and let me baptize you in order to
the remission of your sins " Here comes in the
trouble; Jesus never saves a sinner till he gives
up everything else and utterly abandons himself
to Him. This doctrine of "baptismal remission"

so antagonizes the plan of salvation as to be incompatible with it. So fatal is this heresy of
popery and anticnrist that a man can't receive
it and abide in it without losing his soul. (I
mean the human spirit, *i. e.*, the man proper,
for the heart may give up the water-God and
take Jesus, and still the mind in some sense
hold to the latter).

Whatever comes between the soul and Jesus
is practical. antichrist, *i. e* , takes the place of
Christ and keeps Him from saving you.   Hence,
the man feeling that God is obligated to pardon him in baptism, so he does not, in the
utter abandonment of everything else, cast himself on the mercy of God in Christ, gets no pardon.   Now if he goes on to the end of his life,
thinking his sins were pardoned in baptism, his
heaven will turn out to be hell.

An intelligent Methodist or Baptist earnestly
seeking Jesus may find Him in the water or any-
where else.   But let a man come to the water
deluded by this heresy, that he brings God
under obligation to save him by immersion, he
will come a sinner and go away a sinner, and
never be saved unless he throws away the water-
god and takes Jesus.   I have conversed with
thousands of intelligent, honest people who had

been baptized in order to remission, and have yet to meet the first one who received then and there an intelligent experience of salvation. I have also seen hundreds of them converted at our altars, who testified that they had been deceived. Satan did a land-office business when he raised up the Pope to propagate this doctrine. I doubt whether any other dogma has brought so many souls to hell. The Pope has burnt millions because they wrote and spoke just as I am doing, and he would burn me if he had the power.

But little more than three centuries ago Bishops Latimer and Ridley were chained on opposite sides of the same stake at Smithfield, Eng., and burnt for just what I am now doing. I feel it my duty to write these pages because that heresy is so prevalent in this country, and with the increasing Catholic population is growing. I write against no church. My only desire is that all churches and people should give up error and sin, and take Jesus and holiness.

The water-regenerationists prove their dogma by about as much scripture as you can write on the palm of your hand, all meaning the baptism of the Holy Ghost, which is essential to salvation; but by them misconstrued and applied to

water, thus fortifying all the monstrous papistical pretensions.

Mark xvi . 16, "He that believeth and is baptized, shall be saved," is their chief citadel.
It was the sugar stick of Moses E. Lard all
his life. At Little Hickman, Elder Briney
took it for his first argument, and fought, bled
and died on it.

In the first place, I would simply state that
all the critics of the world have vetoed the
authorship of this text. None of the old and
authoritative manuscripts have it. Tischen-
dorf, the prince of critics, following the Sinaitic
manuscript, the "oldest of all and only one entire," leaves it out altogether.

The latest critical Greek Testament, by Hort
and Westcott, the unanimous concurrence of
universal criticism, gives it, but marks it an in-
terpolation. Thus, like the eunuch's confes-
sion, Acts viii: 37, which they adopted as their
pillar, found to be spurious and discarded by all
authorities, they preach it no more; so Mark
xvi: 16 is in rapid succession to its merited
oblivion. Soon they will preach it no more.

Here is the verdict of all the critics: "It
manifestly can not claim any apostolic authority;
but is doubtless founded on some tradition of

the apostolic age." Hort and Westcott, 2d vol., p. 51, Appendix.

Let me here say that while Mark xvi: 16 is spurious without a doubt, yet I believe it to be in harmony with the word of God. We have the voice of unanimous criticism certifyin ; Mark never wrote it, and it is ''without apostolical authority." Yet it may state a truth, and I believe it does. So let us give it a fair, candid and honest interpretation, "He that believeth and is baptized, shall be saved."

You see there is no water in the text, and I dare say, no man who has not "water on the brain" will ever see it there.

With the Bible before us revealing a baptism for the soul as well as the body, we can easily see which it is. I find the same thing believes, is baptized and is saved. Now, what is that thing? Is it the body or the soul? Can the body believe? You know it can not. Is the body saved? You answer, No. The saint dies as well as the sinner. So what is that thing that believes, is baptized and is saved? You know it is the soul. Hence, you see the plain and simple meaning of the passage is: *The soul believes, the soul is baptized*, and the *soul is saved.* There is no body baptism in it, and never was.

It is in perfect harmony with the uuiform
teaching of the Bible: The sinner believes,
Jesus baptizes him (with the Holy Ghost) and
saves him. Oh! the awful perversion of this passage, used for ages to support the popish doctrine of baptismal regeneration.

ACTS II: 38.

"Repent, and be baptized every one of you, in
the name of Jesus Christ, for the remission of
sins, and ye shall receive the gift of the Holy
Ghost."

I am happy to observe the Revised Version of
1881, which is the most correct English version
extant, omits the Popish phrase "for remission,"
involving conditionality, and very correctly gives
"unto remission," i. e., with reference to or point-
ing to, as water baptism refers to, points to and
emblematizes the baptism of the Holy Ghost, by
which we are saved.

Peter here enforces the baptism of the Holy
Ghost as the salient matter, and so exhorts in
verse 39: "For the promise is to you and to
your children, and to all who are afar off, even
as many as the Lord our God shall call."

As Dean Alford and all the authorities certify
that water baptism here is the outward and
visible sign of the baptism of the Holy Ghost,

he preached Holy Ghost baptism essential and water the symbol referring to it.

These water-regenerationists grossly misrepresent Peter as preaching the essentiality of water baptism, while he lays all the emphasis on the baptism of the Holy Ghost, which they, in order to enthrone their water-god, discard altogether; thus ejecting God from the plan of salvation.

The water-regeneration exegesis of this passage antagonizes all the Bible the above exegesis harmonizes with all the Bible.

Peter's commission, under which he was preaching (Luke xxiv: 47), promising remission of sins on condition of repentance, had no water in it. When Peter preached to the house of Cornelius, the whole congregation were converted, pardoned, regenerated and baptized with the Holy Ghost, and saved without a drop of water.

The cases are parallel. Peter says (Acts xv: 9), on both occasions their hearts were "purified by faith." That is, the gospel. Jesus baptizes and saves, not the preacher.

The water-regenerationists who have debated with me have uniformly denied the baptism of the Holy Ghost altogether since the Apostles, thus dethroning Jesus and enthroning the water-

god. And all this right in the face of Peter in
their favorite Scripture (Acts ii : 39), asserting
that it is for everybody and essential to salvation. Why don't they obey Peter, and when
they baptize with water pray on till Jesus baptizes with the Holy Ghost? They deify the
shadow and reject the substance. So their water-
baptism is solemn mockery, farcical and blasphemous.

ACTS XXII : 16.

"Arise, and be baptized, and wash away thy
sins, calling on the name of the Lord."

Water baptism is the emblem of spirit baptism. Paul's sins were on his soul ; water could
not touch them, unless you adopt the Pagan,
Popish and materialistic heresy of baptismal regeneration and conclude Paul's sins were washed
away by the water. That would do for India or
China, but I don't think you can quite stand it.

Five versions of the New Testament, namely,
Wickliff, Tyndale, Cranmer, Geneva and Rheims,
all render this passage wash away thy sins by
calling on the name of the Lord, i. e., by prayer.
There is no trouble about it. Paul's sins were
symbolically washed away by the water, but
really and actually washed away by the blood of
Christ, the only elixir of purgation, applied by

the Holy Ghost. Could you conclude that the
man who said, "Christ sent me not to baptize,
but to preach the gospel," was a water-regener-
ationist? Paul's commission, under which he
preached all his life, had no water in it. Acts
xxvi: 18.

You remember Paul's watchword: "By deeds
of law shall no flesh be justified." Water baptism
is a deed of the ceremonial law of the gospel
dispensation. So Paul's life-long preaching
irreconcilably refutes baptismal regeneration.

EPH. V: 26.

"That he [Christ] might sanctify and cleanse
it [the church] by the washing of water by the
word." This has been pressed into service by
the waterists. It is so irreconcilable with their
dogma that we will give it but a passing word.
There are two reasons why they can't use this
at all to prove "water baptism in order to remission." One is it is applied to the "church,"
which here is the mystical spiritual body of
Christ. Hence already pardoned and regenerated. The other, it is for sanctification and not
"for remission."

Remission is for sinners, but sanctification is
for Christians only. Hence this can't be for
remission of sins. First, because it is applied

to parties who have no sins to be remitted; and, secondly, because it is not for remission, but for sanctification.

1 PETER III: 20, 21.

"While the ark was preparing, wherein few. *i.e.*, eight souls, were saved by water. The like figure whereunto baptism doth also now save us (not the putting away the filth of the flesh, but the answer of a good conscience toward God)." The clause in this Scripture, "baptism saves us," has been wonderfully vociferated by water-regenerationists.

We don t deny, "baptism saves." But what baptism? Let Peter answer. The adjective and noun, "like figure," in English, is but one word in the Greek, namely, antitupon, *i. e.*, antitype. Throughout the Bible water is a type and Spirit the antitype. So here Peter says the antitype baptism, *i. e.*, the baptism of the Holy Ghost, now saves us. Peter fortifies himself against the very misconstruction the waterists have foisted on him by inserting the parenthetical clause exegetical of his meaning, "not putting away the filth of the flesh," *i. e.*, not water baptism, for the design of water baptism in both Testaments is to remove ceremonial defilement and effect ceremonial purity, while it substantial counterpart (Holy Ghost baptism) removes spiritual defilements and effects spiritual purity. So Peter refutes this heresy by stating, "not the putting away the filth of the flesh, but the answer of a good conscience toward God," *i. e*, the baptism of the Holy Ghost, in which the Spirit applies the atoning blood, washes the heart, makes it whiter than snow. Psalm li: 7.

This Holy Ghost baptism is God's answer to a good conscience, in which he speaks to your soul and tells you your conscience, *i. e.*, your heart, is pure; you are gloriously saved, and saved to the uttermost. This is salvation by baptism sure enough. It is none of your buncombe, supposititious water works.

So be sure you get the "antitype baptism," which Peter says "saves us," *i. e.*, the Holy Ghost baptism saves us and not the type (water).

TITUS III: 5, 6.

"Not by works of righteousness which we have done, but the washing of regeneration and the renewing of the Holy Ghost; which he shed on us abundantly through Jesus Christ our Savior."

I confess my astonishment at the use of this passage by the waterists to support their dogma.

They are demolished at the outset by the very words of Jesus (Matt. iii: 15), "To fulfill all righteousness," in which righteousness is applied to water baptism. When Paul in this text says, "Not by works of righteousness which we have done," it is the same as if he said, not by water baptism.

Again : whatever it was, was poured on them. So if it was baptism, it came by pouring. And that is true. It was the baptism of the Holy Ghost and came by pouring; and so the water symbol (which had no salvation in it, but merely represented salvation) came by pouring.

JOHN III: 5.

"Born of water and of the Spirit."

There is no doubt but this is the water of life, *i. e.*, spiritual water. So thought Calvin, Grotius, Coccieus, Lampe and Tholuck.

This conclusion is confirmed by the fourth and seventh chapters, as well as many other Scriptures in the Old and New Testaments.

The woman at the well in fourth chapter very naturally concluded he meant the water in the well, but she was mistaken. So in vii : 38, he says: "If a man believe in me, out of his belly shall flow rivers of living waters." So we see he meant the Spirit, *i. e.*, the water of life.

Nicodemus, an honest preacher of the gospel, though unconverted, leaped to a Campbellite conclusion, which is perfectly natural to an unconverted man, and said to Jesus: "How can a man be born when he is old? Can he enter the second time into his mother's womb and be born?" He, like all water-remissionists, was a materialist. So he thought our Savior meant a physical birth. This was his blunder, *i. e*, the materiality of the birth in contradistinction to its spirituality. See how sweetly and clearly Jesus corrects him: "That which is born of the flesh is flesh; that which is born of the Spirit is spirit. Marvel not that I said unto you, You must be born from on high," *i. e.*, by the power of God.

Then in verse eighth, by the example of the wind, Jesus proves beyond controversy the pure spirituality of the birth. The waterists all get their feet in Nicodemus' lasso and fall into a mill-pond.

Now what was Nicodemus' blunder? Why it was in thinking Jesus meant a physical birth instead of a spiritual birth, *i. e.*, that his body had to be born again.

Now, you know if water baptism is a birth at all it is a physical birth, *i. e.*, the body is born again. And that is precisely Nicodemus' error, *i. e.*, that his body had to be born again. I do think it is time people would get out of Nicodemus' blunder since our Savior corrected him so fully and clearly. But the reason Nicodemus fell into it was because he was experimentally ignorant of spiritual things. For the same reason Nicodemus' materialistic heresy is preached to-day from so many pulpits.

Every man in the world who has been converted to God knows there is no physical water in the spiritual birth.

If this means water baptism it is only used in a symbolic sense and gives no support to this Popish heresy.

BAPTISM ESSENTIAL.

The reader will understand we frankly admit that baptism is essential to salvation in the highest sense, *i. e*, without it there can be no salvation. But it is the baptism of the Holy Ghost. Now rely upon it, every time the Scriptures recognize baptism essential to salvation it is the baptism of the Holy Ghost.

Be assured, upon a fair exegesis, not a solitary statement in the Bible recognizes water baptism essential to salvation. All this grand pageantry of water regeneration was first Paganism, then Popery, now preached by thousands of Mormon prophets and elders, and minor parties under a diversity of names.

'FAITH ALONE."

Amid the latter day conquests of water theology many orthodox preachers have turned pale at "Faith *a'one*."

I shall be like Luther when the Pope ordered him to exscind it from his theses. He responded No, not to gratify all the Popes in hell—meanwhile they were preparing to burn him. Shame on his weak-kneed gospel sons!

Unconverted preachers in this country for the last forty years have made themselves hoarse ridiculing "faith *alone*."

It is necessary for somebody to defend the truth, and I feel it a sweet privilege.

Every grace in the plan of salvation is unique in its office and signification. We are illuminated by conviction *alone*. The yoke of Satan is broken by repentance *alone*. The yoke of Christ is received by faith *alone*. Sins are blotted out in justification *alone*. The new life is imparted by regeneration *alone*. The old life is taken away by sanctification *alone*.

Now no one is so silly as to think any one of these graces excludes the rest. Yet in this sense

3

has this Popish howl been rung from hundreds
of so-called Protestant pulpits for the last half
century.

In the exclusive sense in which they accuse
us of holding this doctrine none but a few Anti-
nomian fanatics ever did hold it. Don't you
know justification and sanctification by "faith
alone," are the point of departure from Roman-
ism—the salient point and cardinal doctrine of
all the Protestants? Jesus is our prophet, priest
and king—he "*alone*" is the Savior. "Faith
alone" is the human side—Christ "alone" the
divine side. If one is true the other is true.

This fight against "faith alone" is nothing but
the old war of Antichrist, i. e., rivalry and antagonism to Christ. I don't wonder Satan hates
"faith alone;" for it dethrones the Pope, kills
the water-god and all of his idols, and is des-
tined to conquer the world for Christ. There
has never been a soul saved by any other doctrine. Reader, have you been saved? If so, I
venture to say it was just when you threw away
all your own righteousness—such as your moral
virtues, good works, water baptism, etc., and
took Christ as your only and all-sufficient
Savior.

Now, don't you know you took Christ by

"faith alone?" Faith is the only receptive grace. Hence you can't receive Christ by anything but faith, *i. e.*, "faith alone." If you don't take Christ alone as your Savior you are lost forever. When you cast everything away and receive Christ alone, then you exercise "faith alone."

I can easily see how unconverted men can preach against "faith alone" But this I do know, that no Christian can intelligently argue against "faith alone," because he knows he was saved just in that way, by letting go the ship and walking out, like Peter on the water, by "faith alone." All anybody ever did or has to do to be saved is to give up sin and Satan and receive Jesus, which is done by "faith alone."

For authority for this doctrine I refer you to the Bible from Alpha to Omega. In the New Testament alone I can give you five hundred texts proving this doctrine.

Of course my space is limited; but as I said in the Preface, it will afford me great pleasure to meet any man endorsed by his people in oral discussion, if he desires to controvert these doctrines.

ACTS XVI: 31:

" Believe on the Lord Jesus Christ and thou shalt be saved."

Elder Briney, at Little Hickman, acknowledged that this passage, as well as many others
quoted, taught justification by "faith alone," if
"isolated and independent." I then and now con-
tend that this and hundreds of others are "isolated and independent."

The case of the jailer is demonstrative and
incontrovertible. To say he was not saved by
"faith alone" is to flatly contradict Paul. The
trembling sinner asks, "What must I do to be
saved?" The answer comes promptly: "Believe on the Lord Jesus Christ and thou shalt
be saved." Paul tells him nothing but "believe." If anything else was necessary Paul
stands in the attitude of a falsifier. But Paul
told him true; for he was saved then and there.
The reason people are not saved now is because
men don't preach to them the straight, clear,
simple gospel: "Believe and ye shall be saved,"
but they are befogged with human policy, *i. e.*
Popery. Will any one dare say this is not an
"isolated and independent" statement? So, as
Elder Briney acknowledged, it proves indis-
putably justification by "faith alone."

If you want to see people saved by thousands
go back to the good old Pauline Wesleyan doctrine of justification and sanctification by "faith
alone."

This false Popish doctrine has transformed the church (the Lord's panoplied army) into hospitals of sick (unsanctified Christians) and dead people (unconverted sinners). Hence the distressing inefficiency of preachers and churches. Abandon your Popery, salvation by works, cry "Behold the Lamb of God that taketh away the sins of the world," and Jesus will come and work miracles of grace.

JAMES II: 24.

"You see, then, how that by works a man is justified, and not by faith only."

This passage is forever quoted by the Papists. There are four justifications: that of the infant without faith or works; that of the sinner by "faith only;" that of the Christian by faith and works, and that of the final judgment by works only.

Here James speaks of a Christian, Abraham, forty-one years after he had been justified when a sinner by "faith alone," as Paul so abundantly teaches. Every Christian is justified by works, not in sense of pardon, but approval.

PHIL. II: 12, 13.

"Work out your salvation with fear and trembling, for it is God that worketh in you to will and to do of his good pleasure."

This is spoken to Christians with reference
to grace culture, and gives no support to the
Papistical heresies of "salvation by works."
"For it is God that worketh in you to will and
to do of his good pleasure."
The plain meaning is, you abandon yourself
to God unreservedly by "faith alone;" you turn
your will over to him unconditionally and abide
in perfect submission forever. He takes you
and sanctifies you; takes your will into hand,
so you have no longer your own will, but God's
will. Meanwhile God transforms your will in
such a way that when you put forth volitions
they are in perfect harmony with God's will.
Self is crucified; your will is lost in God's will.
Still you are free and exercise your own sanctified will; so sanctified as to be identified with
God's will. In that case you are a great worker;
for God has something for you to do all the
time, and you can't be idle. We work like tools.
"God works in us, of his own good pleasure."
Reader, this is sweet and delightful work.
Angels love to do this work. Are you happy in
the Lord's vineyard?
  This is the Lord's sweet work; but work as a
condition of pardon is Satan's work. It is done
by none but Satan's people and always in his

kingdom, and of course it belongs to him. When the devil can get a sinner to seek salvation by works he is sure to get him if he don't get his eyes open, see the utter futility of all his works and give himself to Jesus by "faith alone." It is a great pity the gospel has been so obscured by this heresy. It is everywhere keeping people from Jesus and salvation.

Interview every Christian you meet and he will tell you he was saved just when he gave up all his works and took Jesus by "faith alone." The same is true of sanctification. It is always by "faith alone."

Paul says (Rom. iv: 16): "It is by faith, that it may be by grace [free gift]; that the promise might be sure to all the seed." So the very economy of grace requires it to be by "faith alone." O! how happy this world would be if they would throw down the devil's trash and take Jesus.

Do you want pardon? Let everything else go and receive it at the hands of Jesus by "faith alone," or you will never get it. Do you want sanctification? Throw away Satan's lie that you get it by works, and so must wait to do the works. "Reckon yourselves to be dead indeed unto sin, but alive unto God" (Rom. vi ·

11). And while you reckon it God will make
it so and give you the joyous experience certified by the Holy Spirit, "sanctified wholly."

This false Popish doctrine of remission in
water baptism has thrown its pestiferous branches
over Kentucky and portions of the adjoining
States like a deadly Upas tree for the last forty
years. The result is all denominations have
been affected by the malaria.

Twenty years ago the Baptists and Presby-
terians all had their altars and got the people
converted and received them on their experi-
ences. Now they have no altars. Consequently
they have no fire to burn up the sins of the
people. Hence they take them in on a dry, cold
profession of faith, without satisfactory evidences
of conversion.

The Methodists have lamentably given up
their altars, let the fire go out and religion die,
and sadly drifted back to the cold, dead level of
Episcopal ritualism—class-meetings dead and
sanctification forgotten.

Brethren, don't you know we are to-day living
in a North-pole atmosphere? It is, at least in
part, imputable to the propagation of baptismal
regeneration. It is an Arctic iceberg stranded
in our midst and chilling the entire atmosphere

down to the zero point. If all the Methodists will rally around our altars God will pour down fire from heaven and melt this iceberg. Rally, rally!

Don't you know, brethren, the altar is mentioned four hundred times in the Bible? Don't you know we insult God when we give it up? Why is religion dead and dying in so many of our churches? It is for the want of the baptism of the Holy Ghost and fire. Fire to burn up the sins of the people and the Holy Ghost to regenerate and sanctify. Preach justification and sanctification by faith alone and you will run the devil; for faith alone is the antithesis of Christ alone, and leaves out the devil, the Pope, the water-god and all human trash, and gives Christ all the glory. Call the people to the altar. Make all your members pray, confess and testify, throw away all carnal and time-serving policy, and preach the truth fearless of men and devils, and God will pour down his Spirit and emblazon the whole country with the lightnings of perpetual Pentecost.

GOOD-BYE.

Now, little book, I have written you with an eye single to the glory of God, guided and illuminated by his blessed Holy Spirit. Go and

preach the gospel to the thousands who have
heard my voice, but will never hear it again
till we meet in glory, and to the myriads who
have never heard my voice; and the blessing of
the Father, Son and Holy Ghost go with you
and use you to destroy error, enforce truth, con-
vict, convert and sanctify souls.

THE END.

APPENDIX.

The preceding book was written by your humble servant twenty-five years ago, at the close of my ten years' war with Campbellites, who having provoked the war and driven me into the conflict, despite all of my convictions to the contrary; as I was so busy preaching the everlasting gospel and saving souls by hundre.'s and thousands, God condescending to use my humble instrumentality, that I resisted as long as I could, till one of their champions, after repeatedly challenging me through the mail, having come to my revival and witnessed thronging multitudes and crowded altars seeking and finding the Lord; among them some of his own members, passing triumphantly from death unto life, brilliantly testifying to the power of the Holy Ghost to convert and save, and at the same time witnessing to their sad delusions, depending on the water god.

At this crisis, asking permission to speak, w ich I freely granted, he certified that he had repeatedly challenged me in writing which I had utterly ignored; then in presence of the multitude he repeated all of his challenges, certifying that I was preaching error and leading the people astray.

Thus he forced me into the war, which like
the siege of old Troy, lasted ten years; meanwhile they called into the fight their champions from the ends of the earth; the one having
led off the battle, though an old debater, retreating, crestfallen, from the field and return-
ing no more. During the conflict they constantly weakened, till no champion could be
found and the battle-field became silent. The
heroism they manifested richly deserved a
better cause; but the water-god incontestibly
demonstrated the pertinancy of his cognomen,
"weak as water." They began boldly affirming immersion, thus heroically wielding the
laboring oar. Long before the bloody decade
came to a close, I stood constantly in the front
affirming affusion, till they all retreated from
the field.

CHAPTER I.

THE APOSTOLIC PRACTICE—AFFUSION ONLY.

In the providence of God I have traveled in the Holy Land, Egypt, Syria, Greece and Italy in 1895, 1899 and 1905, carefully examining everything that can throw light on the apostolic practice, signally failing to find a solitary trace of immersion, but everywhere finding overwhelming confirmations of the uniform Bible testimony to affusion. John's baptism was all affusion, as he and Jesus abundantly testify. Mark 1:8; Luke 3:16; Acts 1:5 and 11:16 all certify positively that John handled the water and not the people. In these four passages we have *hudati* (water) without a preposition which is the regular dative of instrumentality, showing positively as John and Jesus both certify in these passages that he handled the water, and not the people; *i. e.* just as you say "a man walks with a staff," or "chops with an axe," or "colors the house with paint." Besides, the Jordan at that place is fifteen feet deep in low water; the banks steep and sudden offset, and the current so very swift that a man can not stand in it. When I was there in 1905, the three Texas boys, my traveling companions, con-

strained me to immerse them. Our noble
guide, Shukrey Hishmeat, a native of Jerusalem, forty years old, having all his life served
as guide, and I trow the best one in the whole
country; though an Arab, a noble Christian,
positively forbade me to immerse them, alleging with much excitement and flowing tears,
that "he had seen men drown there." Then
the Texas boys, who swim like ducks, at once
relieved him of all responsibility. Consequently he had only to take care of me in the
modus operandi. I several times walked to and
fro hunting a good place to get into water
deep enough to immerse them (as the river
flows so swiftly, stirring up the black mud and
darkening the water till you can not see an
inch below the surface.) When I waded down
through mud half way up to my knees, exercising the utmost care lest I slip down and the
current carry me away, both the guide and
our armed escort accompanied me, holding me
fast lest I got drowned, in which case their responsibility would have been heavy, as I had
not relieved them. When I got in position
the Texas boys swam to me and I administered
the ordinance of immersion, letting them go
and swim out at liberty. For John to have
immersed all those people in that precipitous,
swelling flood was a physical impossibility;
besides, he positively certifies that he did not
do it, but handled the water instead of the people. All the statuary and engravings, and

sculptures found in the catacombs of Rome
and elsewhere, represent Jesus standing, and
John pouring water on His head.
Matthew, Mark and Luke all certify Jesus referring to John's baptism as His authority for
exercising the sarcedotal office; showing that
John did to Him with water just as Moses did
to Aaron when he poured the oil on his head:
as the baptism of Jesus by John was His annointing for the priesthood, *i. e.*, his public
inauguration into His official Messiahship. If
John had not done to the people with water
the very thing that Jesus did to the people
with the Holy Ghost, he would have been under the necessity to use a different word;
whereas he constantly used that native Greek
word, baptize, which invariably designates
the great saving work of Christ, which he ad-
ministers by affusion only. Acts chapters 2
and 11. If John had immersed the people, he
would have said *katapontizoo*. Matt. 14:30; 18:6;
or *buthizoo*. I Tim. 5:9.

Both of these words mean immerse and are
used in the New Testament. If John or any
one else had immersed, he would certainly
have used one of these words. But the very
fact that they are used in the New Testament
and never for baptism a single time is demonstrative truth that they did not immerse. All
honest Bible readers know that the baptisms
administered by our Savior are all afiusions.
John the Baptist and all the apostles con-

stantly certify that they did the same thing
with water that Jesus did with the Holy Ghost
and fire. Rest assured they told the truth, for
they were inspired of God. It was utterly impossible for them to reveal an immersion in
water and an affusion with the Holy Ghost
without using different words. That the Pentecostal baptisms were simply the Jewish
affusions which they had practiced constantly
from the days of Moses, is a matter of fact,
as clearly revealed by the inspired Word and
corroborated so abundantly by the environ-
ments, as to be utterly indisputable by all honest Bible readers, who are free from that formidable disease which Jesus alone can heal,
i. e., hydrocephalus, i. e., weter on the brain.
Glory to His name, He healed me when He
baptized me wi+h the Holy Ghost and fire nineteen years after I had forced a Methodist
preacher to immerse me in water, to satisfy
my longing soul so hungry for the fulness of
God. I have been in Jerusalem in June, the
time the Pentecostal revival swept down from
heaven converting three thousand in the
morning and five thousand in the afternoon
all of whom were baptized without any separate appointment, showing clearly that it was
the simple Jewish affusion, which Moses administered to the three millions of Israel when
he sprinkled them all at the tabernacle door,
upon the ratification of the Sinaic covenant
in the wilderness; which is called baptism in

v. 10 (see my version.) There was actually no immersion water nearer than the Jordan, fifty miles, the city being supplied with water from the Pools of Solomon, twelve miles distant, in which they were not allowed to immerse, if they had gone thither, but they did not go, as you know the meetings moved directly on. Baptism is an Old Testament institution, practiced super-aboundingly and incessantly from the days of Moses, and simply continued with great eliminations in the gospel dispensation, beautifully symbolizing the glorious work of Christ in the expurgation of the human heart, pouring on us in copious affusion the Holy Ghost and fire.

When a boy I have often heard the Campbellites preach on the baptism of the enuch by Phillip, in their estimation proving immersion; thus, simply demonstrating that with water on the brain one can see rivers and oceans *ad libitum.* I have six times been at that place. It is eighteen miles on the road leading south from Jerusalem to Gaza. It is simply a water-spout shooting out of the rock about one inch in diameter, so highly appreciated in that land celebrated for scarcity of water, that if you ever see it you will recognize it long before you get there by a group of a dozen women, standing, each waiting her turn to put the mouth of her water-pot under the spout and hold it till it runs full. No stream flows from it, as the water is all used; the

herds and flocks so glad to get what little the
people leave. This is known throughout that
country as "Phillip's Fountain," as there he
baptized the Ethiopian enuch. Bedeken's
Guide Book, the authority for all of that country, thus certifying.

Thus in the providence of God, having three
times been permitted to explore that country,
I find no reason to change a solitary word in
my book which I wrote from the Bible alone
thirteen years before I ever saw the places recorded in the inspired history. I find the Land
and the Book, thus in perfect harmony, both
alike, robbing the water-god of his glory and
giving it all to Jesus.

CHAPTER II.

THE LATIN BIBLE.

God raised up Alexander the Great and gave him all the world B. C. 325. Of course, he put the Greeks in every government under heaven; the normal result in the roll of generations developing the universal dissemination of that beautifnl and wonderful Greek language wh'ch had become universal, thus the indispensable preparation for the evangelization of the world. Our Saviour and His apostles all preached and wrote in that language.

The Romans conquered the Jews 70 B. C., giving great promise to their language, and actually achieved the conquest of the whole world at the time the nations were thrilled by the Star of Bethlehem proclaiming the advent of the world's Redeemer. Under this universal Roman rule, the Latin language rapidly gained the ascendancy over the Greek, bringing out the translation of the Holy Scriptures into that language into the second century, contemporary with the Apostle John and the Christian Fathers and recognized as having the apostolic endorsement.

Whereas baptism is a pure Greek word and

consequently does not appear in the Old Testament, unless you take Septuagint, which is the Greek translation, which was made B. C. 280. But immersion is a pure Latin word and would most assuredly appear in the Latin Bible as a translation of the Greek baptisma if it had that meaning. The simple fact that it is now nowhere used for baptism in the Latin Bible, is incontestable demonstrative proof that it is not the meaning of the word. The English language this day has 150,000 words, whereas only 23,000 are original; thus five-sixths of the language having been adopted from an endless diversity of exotics. The translators simply Latinized the Greek *baptidzo*, thus adopting it into the Latin language, rather than translating it; meanwhile they had their own native word immerse at their command, which integrity would have forced them to use, if the apostolic practice had been immersion. This is an argument which they will never answer. God forbid that they should be dishonest enough to evade it, in order to promote idolatry in the worship of the water-god which is the most formidable phase of idol worship in all Christendom.

CHAPTER III.

KING JAMES' TRANSLATION.

Was made by forty-seven men in 1611, called together by this monarch for that noble work. The Dark Ages which followed the fall of Rome A. D. 476 and lasted a thousand years, during which not one man in a thousand, nor one woman in twenty thousand could read or write were just drifting away and retreating before the rising sun of Christian civilzation which was signally accelerated by the discovery of America. The revival of learning, the invention of the art of printing, and the Lutheran reformation, which dawned under Wickliffe A. D. 1380, continuing under John Huss and his followers and culminating under the wonderful preaching of the Austine monk, actually developing into the glorious sunburst of the Protestant church.

During these long and dreary thousand years, Satan's millennium, the black midnight of time; literature was almost exterminated from the earth, there being no schools to perpetuate it; barbarians ruling every nation. Theref're this translation was really a wonder for its time, as there was so little learning

in all the earth. During the dark ages the
uniform practice was trine immersion in a
state of nudity; the preachers serving the men
and deaconesses the women, divesting them of
every stitch of clothing (alleging that there
was no authority for baptizing clothing), im-
merging them three times in a state of utter
nudity, in the name of the Father, Son and
Holy Ghost, calling each person of the Trinity
with each separate immersion, consequently
the translators had all been immersed three
times, believing that it was the apostolic
mode.

Therefore, you see they were badly water-
logged, all having that fatal disease, hydrocephalus, i. e. water on the brain. Therefore,
they copiously watered their translation, thus
leading millions, and among them your humble servant, into rivers and lakes. The people
get immersed and say it is because they want
to follow Jesus "into the water and out
again;" whereas it does not say went into it,
and though it says He came up out of it, it is
a well known fact that *apo* does not mean out
of, but from; thus implying that John's meetings were held on the Jordan. He preached
and baptized in the wilderness, where there
was no immersion water, till the accumulation
of the multitud s needed so much water that
he moved his meet ngs to the Jordan, just as
we hold a great camp-meeting where there is
an abundant supply of water for men and ani-

mals. It is utterly impossible for a Greek
scholar to prove that they ever went into the
water, or came out of it, as the words used by
the Holy Ghost are perfectly satisfied by the
translation, "went to the water," and "came
from it;" whereas in many instances, e. g. Peter
at the house of Cornelius speaks of bringing
the water to baptize them, instead of taking
them to it, as *to hudor*, the water, is the subject of *kolusai*, to move. The same is true
when Annanias baptized Saul of Tarsus in the
house of Judas on Straight street in Damas-
cus. I have been in it, there is no immersion
water nearer than the river Abana, to which
they did not go; as Annanias simply told him
to stand up and receive baptism.

Dr. Dowie believes the trine immersion was
the apostolic practice. In this he is mistaken,
as it is utterly impossible to find a trace of immersion before the third century. In that
centuryLactantius, the oldest historian, gives
us a clear record appertaining to the apostolic
practice: "*iohanes tinxit, petrus tinxit, et Chris-
tus misit apostolous, ut gentes tingerent.*" "John
the Baptist sprinkled, Peter sprinkled, and
Christ sent his apostles that they should
sprinkle the nations " This author as you
see, wrote in Latin. Since immerse is a Latin
word, it is absolutely certain that he would
have used it, if it had been the apostolic practice, but he certifies as you see that they all
sprinkled, which is in beautiful harmony with

the Bible. Ez. 36:25. "I will sprinkle clean water on you," and Isa. 52:15, "So shall he sprinkle many nations." These prophecies have their fulfilment in the gospel dispensation, showing that the mode of Baptism, which was invariably affusion, in the former dispensation, was not changed under the gospel. Many a godly Jew was baptized thousands and myriads of times under the law as they received it every time they contracted ceremonial defilement, to which they were incessantly exposed, coming in contact with unclean animals, lepers. dead bodies, and even Gentiles.

As our dispensation is purely and preeminently spiritual, once in life is sufficient to symbolize the perpetual work of the Holy Spirit, purifying the heart.

Baptize has but one meaning in the Bible, and that is to purify. John 3:25, if you will read the context, it will perfectly satisfy you on the subject, as it positively defines baptism to be a purification. You find the same definition clearly and positively given, Luke 11:5, 7-9. In this case Jesus, responsive to the invitation of a Pharisee to dine with him, goes in and sits down at the table without washing his hands. Responsive to the criticism of his host He observes,

"You Pharisees make clean the outside of the cup and the plate, while the interior is full of extortion and impurity, therefore make clean

the interior and you are all clean." The word
in this passage translated wash in E. V. is *baptidzo*, which is constantly used for baptism.
Therefore you see (my version) that *katharizo*
is the literal and unequivocal difinition of
baptidzo.

You will not dare go back on this passage as
the Savior Himself is the author of it, clearly
and unequivocally defining baptize by the
very word which means purify throughout the
Bible.

Mark 7:4. we have *rantizoo* (to sprinkle) used
interchangeably and synonymously with *baptidzo*. We also have the same in Rev. 19:13,
where our Savior is described as a mounted
warrior, leading his armies in the great battle
of Armageddon, and his garments sprinkled
with the blood, splashed on them as he sat on
His horse and pressed the conflict to the gate
of the enemy. There we have *bebammenon*
i e. the perfect participle for *baptoo*, used
synonymously with *rerammenon*, the participle
from *rantizoo*, to sprinkle.

Hence you see in these passages the native
word baptize, in the inspired Greek, generally
means to purify and specifically to sprinkle in
order to the purification which was the current practice among the Jews from the days
of Moses, with no intimation of a change in
the New Testament dispensation.

CHAPTER IV.

THE DICTIONARIES.

It is pertinent to observe that the immersionists rely solely on the dictionaries, the errors in King James, which they inserted inadvertently bending it to their own opinions, which had been developed by the uniform pratice of trine immersion during the long roll of the dark ages, and the misinterpretation of Romans 6th chapter and Col. 2.

While baptism has but one Bible definition, i. e. a purification including the great expurgatory works of the Holy Ghost in regeneration and sanctification ritualistically symbolized by the simple affusion of pure water on the body; homogeniously with the annointing for bodily healing, James 5:14, the oil symbolizing the Holy Ghost as healer of the body, similitudiously to the water which symbolizes Him as purifier of the heart. In this passage we are clearly fortified against the idolatrous conclusion that the oil heals, as we have a clear statement "the prayer of faith shall save the sick," the oil merely symbolizing the work of the Holy Ghost as the watery baptism emblemetizes His mighty work in regeneration and sanctification. I have anointed

many for healing, simply putting a drop of
the oil on the body, having never yet found a
person who desired immersion in a tank of oil.
The case of water baptism is precisely parallel
while the Greek *baptidzoo* is generic, simply
meaning to purify; yet it is satisfied with any
application of water, whether immersion,
affusion or aspersion. The great standard lexicons give immerse, as a prominent meaning
of the word, but certify that it is never used
in this sense in the New Testament but in that
of affusion. You will find this defiinition
clearly and elaborately given in the great lex-
icon of Rev. John Schlensner, D D. This dictionary expository of New Testament Greek
consists of two large volumes, the full size of
a margin Bible, than which there is no higher
authority on the earth. You will find the
same in Robinson, which is currently used by
all English speaking nations. While *baptidzo*
in Pagan Greek sometimes means immerse,
the highest lexical authority certifies that it
is never used in this sense in the New Testament; but that of simple affusion, symbolizing
the outpouring of the Holy Spirit, in the baptism which Jesus gives to every truly consecra-
ted, believing soul and is certified the *sine qua
non* without which no one shall see the Lord.
Heb. 12;14.

The Bible is its own dictionary, giving but
one definition to *baptidzo*, and that is to purify,
John 3:25, and Luke 11:57-60, I Peter 3:18-22.

and really all other passages where the word occurs. If we were to follow the Pagan Greek we would utterly ruin the New Testament. The Greeks were an exceedingly religious people, having in the Alexandrian conquests actually adopted all the gods worshiped by the nations of the earth and honored them with temples and shrines; and meanwhile fearing lest they might be leaving out some god whom they knew not, they had erected on the Acropolis at Athens a shrine which they dedicated "to the unknown god." Paul availed himself of this open door to preach to them the true God in that memorable day on the Acropolis Acts 17th chapter. Now, suppose you interpret *theos* (god) according to the analogy of the immersionists on *baptidzo*, you would actually have no God in the Bible but the Greek idols, as this word in ninety-nine cases out of every hundred simply meant their idols, which they believed to be gods.

When the Greek language became the vehicle of inspired truth, words eliminated old Pagan meanings, and delectably amplified, intensified and beautified, inherent significations which had somewhat slumbered, occult amid the dark shadows of idolatry till emancipated out of heathen superstitions they became the luminous electric cars, with lightning velocity transmitting the saving truth of God to the benighted millions, sitting in darkness and the shadow oi death.

Whereas it is utterly impossible to find in the inspired word a trace or a track of immersion; its Paganistic origin is clear and indisputable. Among the heathen idols no divinity receives a larger share of their devotions than the water-god. In India they devoutly worship the holy Ganges and Jumna, even ejecting their own children into the swelling floods as a votive offering of the truly pious parents to their gods, which the British government is now heroically endeavoring to prohibit by law. While traveling on those rivers I constantly saw the people immersing to wash away their sins, so vividly reminding me of the Campbellites and Mormons in my own country. They, however, more consistent than our American friends, repeat the immersion indefinitely as they have no way to get rid of their sins, consequently they are always going in to wash them away. As India is a great country and multiplied millions live too remote to avail themselves of the salvatory immersions in these holy waters, they have constructed great public tanks in all parts of the country not blessed by those sacred rivers; the Brahmin priests consecrating them and thus imparting the power to wash away sins. In Madras, the largest city in South India, the holy tank occupies a whole square confronted by three streets, one side being occupied by the great Pantheon in which all the gods of India are worshiped. This tank is beautifully and elegantly built of nicely hewn stone and entered by flights of steps from the four sides, thus affording ample accommodations for thousands of pilgrims, simultaneously to descend and wash their sins away. The heathen in all ages have thus practiced the entire immersion of the body to wash away their sins. When Constantine the Emperor was converted to Christianity A. D. 321, he became exceedingly enthusiastic, traveling throughout his world-wide empire and doing his utmost to compel all people to become Christians. As great Rome, with her four millions of people was crowded with Pagan temples, which he labored in vain to convert to Christianity, largely succeeding, but utterly unable to effect a complete evangelization of the world's capital and metropolis, consequently he transferred the capitol to Constantinople, where he was enabled to carry out his favorite policy of a solid Christian city to represent his universal empire, and co-operate with him in the world's evangelization.

The result of his indefatigable efforts was the conversion of almost all the world on a plain so depreciated spiritually as to admit the Pagan millions; priests everywhere turning preachers, and the Paganistic churches turning Christian, nominally and professionally, real experimental, personal salvation being the exception to the general rule; the normal effect of which was to Paganize the church, and develop Greek and Roman Catholicism: this day with their three hundred and fifty millions, occupying the intermediate plain between Paganism and Christianity. As the heathen in all ages have practiced immersion in water to wash away their sins. As a normal consequence when the Pagan millions poured into the church they brought immersion with them, which never had been practiced among Jews and Christians for baptism, but the simple affusion, which rings throughout both Testaments; while the word immersion is a total stranger to Bible phraseology.

CHAPTER V.

Why Do You Immerse People?

Simply to satisfy their consciences. I Peter 3:21, and like Paul "that I may be all things to all men, in order to save some." When the Lord sanctified me in 1868, He made me a cyclone fire, and I had revivals everywhere, multitudes of people getting eonverted and joining the churches.

In this country, so terribly water-logged by the errors in King James' translation, it was easier to immerse them all to their satisfaction than to preach them out of the water. Besides, I could not have a clear conscince and quit preaching the gospel, which is "the power of God unto salvation," Rom. 1:15, and go to preaching on water, which never did have any thing to do with salvation; acquiescently saying with Paul, I Cor. 1:17, "Christ sent me not to baptize, but to preach the gospel." Oh, the infinite value of the precious time and golden opportunities which Ame ican preach ers have wasted expounding water problems! How grievous to the Holy Spirit, who is so anxious to have all come to a knowledge of the truth and be saved ! Preaching the gospel is God's institution for the salvation of souls.

Let us lose no opportunity and fool away no

time talking about water, wood, stone or anything else that never did have anything to do
with salvation, which is a pure spirituality
and utterly independent of the material world.
Teaching is not for salvation but for the edi-
fication of saved people. Hence it is the
crowning glory of the evangelical school which
Jesus inaugurated and taught three years, and
now under the auspices of the great holiness
movement, bedecking every sky and is accumulating new stars continually to light every
nation to find and joyfully appreciate the
King's highway of holiness. These Bible
schools which constitute the crowning glory of
this most enlightened age the world has ever
seen, can not with impunity ignore any Bible
truth. Therefore, we dare not spare the
water-god any longer. While, of course, immersion does not commit you to the water-god,
yet it normally trends that way by magnify-
ing the ordinance, and as an inevitable conse
quence minifying Christ, who must be all and
in all if you take passage on the old Ship of
Zion and steer clear of the seductive whirl-
pools, the Scylla of wild fanaticism on the one
side and the Charybdis of idolatry on the
other. Hydrolatry, *i. e.*, water worship, is the
idolatry most fatal to the Protestant churches.
Campbellites and Mormons, and some others,
unblushingly preaching immersion in order to
the remission of sins, are downright hydrola-
trers.

Peter had no trouble to walk on the stormy sea of Galilee until he got his eye on the water, when he began to sink. Shall we not profit by his example? I have known not a few holiness people, get immersed, become stickleristical, leak out, and backslide; the water having put out the fire. At that point God in great mercy delivered me when an ignorant youth led astray by preachers, "wise above what is written" and "having a zeal not according to knowledge:" I resorted to the water-god, but finding him "weak as water," I left him forever and began to climb Mount Zion. As I had no guide, it took me nineteen years to reach the Pentecostal summit, where the fire fell, burning up the Free Mason, the Odd Fellows, the College President, the candidate for the Episcopacy, and the Methodist preacher, and leaving me no leader but Jesus, no guide but the Holy Ghost, and no authority but God's word.

Nineteen hours, environed by the cloud of witnesses which this day shake the earth with their heroic tread, would have sufficed me as well as the nineteen years I groped in the absence of living witnesses to entire sanctification and the fulness of God, which I sought in immersion and everything else I could think of, but found at last in Jesus only. God has permitted me to travel extensively and know many of His dear people. My observation is that the people who magnify ordinances are in no case the brightest exemplars of spirituality. Big baptisms, sacraments, full houses, pipe organs, tall steeples, paid choirs, human creeds and institutions all conduce to despiritualize the church and prepare the people for a backsliders' hell.

The greatest objection to immersion consists in the fact that its advocates pervert the word of God, robbing Jesus of His glory, and turning it over to the water-god.

In Rom. 6th chap. and Col. 2d chap. we have the plain simple statement of Old Adam's crucifixion and destruction in every saved soul, and his interment into the death of Christ, which is the vicarious substitutionary atonement, in which the "old man" of sin in every heart must be buried forever or that soul, with this ponderous mill stone around the neck will sink eternally into a bottomless hell.

Crucifixion under Roman law was precisely what hanging is among Anglo Saxons. When the law executes the criminal, it never does leave the body unburied. Here you see baptism is both the sheriff and the undertaker who crucified the "old man" of sin and buries him into the death of Christ, so deep that Satan's resurrection trumpet will never reach him.

To impute this stupendous work to the immersion of the physical body, is puerile, and bordering on blasphemy, and the presumption that it has any such power, the climax of absurdity.

Nothing but the baptism with the Holy Ghost and fire which Jesus gives can effect these results. You know~ the mode of that baptism is affusion. The ordinance of water symbolizes it, which can only be done by pouring or sprinkling. All of that favorite theory constantly preached by immersionists that you must get immersed to symbolize the death and burial of our Lord is utterly gratuitous; water baptism having no such a significance; its office being to symbolize the work of the Holy Spirit in regeneration and sanctification; while the Lord' Supper symbolizes His death, burial and resurrection. All of this clamor that water baptism is a burial is without a solitary word of support from the alpha to the omega of inspired truth, but flatly contrdictory of the plain statement that we are buried by baptism.

Here baptism is the agent which crucifies the "old man" and buries him into the atonement.

Therefore it is not the baptism but one of the works wrought by baptism, and is the normal concomitant of the crucifixion, as the government always buries the corpse when it executes criminals.

In Col. 2d chap. there you see the burial is in logical and grammatical apposition with the circumcision made "without hands." We have a rule in the grammars; "nouns in apposition mean the same thing." As this is circumcision made without hands, you know it is a purely spiritual operation, and means none other than the crucifixion of the "old man." Romans 6:6.

"Now, Brother Godbey, as you so clearly prove that immersion is unknown in the Bible, Paganistic in its origin, indefensible in the Scriptures, conducing to spoliate our blessed Christ of His glory and turn it over to the water-god; meanwhile its normal trend is to despiritualize and lead to hydrolatry, the most prevalent idolatry in the Protestant churches: therefore do you not think you make a mistake in administering it?"

I must answer this question most positively in the negative While we dare not fail to sound the trumpet along all danger lines, and that incessantly, we must allow great liberti s on all non-essentials, i. e., ordinances and churchisms of every kind.

God has made plenty of water and is not stingy with it. Therefore give everybody all he wants; at the same time heroically teaching him that nothing but the blessed Omn'potent Christ has anything to do with saving a soul.

On essentials, i. e.. salvation full and free by Christ alone we dare not compromise one iota. On non essentials lay no embargo, but let every one walk in his own light; at the same time always doing your best to give them the full light of God's Wo'd, Spirit and Providence. God bless every reader.

Round Trip
$1.00

Just think of it! You can go to Palestine, visit all the Bible country and principal places of interest in a few hours for only One Oollar!

Send us the amount and you and your children and your preacher can take the trip with Rev. F. M. Hill, in his book, "To Palestine and Back With The Children."

This book is written to interest the young as well as the old. It contains 212 pages, printed on fine laid paper, large, clear type, and has thirty-six beautiful pictures, illustrating the trip: neatly bound in fine silk cloth: stamped in gold: $1.00 post paid.

Pentecostal Pub. Co., Louisville, Ky.